Excel for Everyone

A Guide that doesn't call you a Dummy

By

RODERICK EDWARDS

Copyright © 2020

rodericke.com/excelall

INTRODUCTION

With all the self-help Excel books on the market you chose this one because you aren't anyone's dummy. Whether you are new to Excel or have many years of experience, this book will help you quickly and easily leverage skills and tips that will have you working with it like a pro.

My over 20 years' experience in a variety of industries including a training supervisor at a telecom company with over 400 employees will help me relate the material in a hopefully easy to learn manner with a bit of humor...as cracked as my humor may be.

If I were launching into my "trainer mode", I'd be telling you what I expect you to learn from this book but then again, shouldn't that be obvious from the title? Anyhow, this book is structured in a specific way to help you move right along into the next concept. How do I know? Because had someone written a book like this, it wouldn't have taken me so long to understand Excel. Like you, I don't want to read some massive reference guide that looks like a novel or try to decipher some nerd-speak. So, let's get to it!

TABLE OF CONTENTS

DEDICATION

I wrote this book for all the people who not only asked me to make some spreadsheet or code some VBA macro, but for all the people who will be asking you to do that when you're done with this book.

A special thanks to Don Huskey, Dawn Curry, Brandon Fisher, Perla Hutchinson Flores, and many others over the years who have pushed me to create "*magic*".

CHAPTER 1 PROCESS THINKING

The first thing to doing anything is realizing it is a process like any other process. Whether you are making cupcakes or launching rockets, everything is a matter of following steps. If you can associate steps or processes, you can do most anything. Don't get caught up on the details or the impact of whatever it is you are trying to accomplish. Just lay out the process in your head. Step 1… Step 2… and on and on. One of the keys to learning Excel is not how to type into little rectangular boxes but rather thinking in a "bullet-pointed" manner. Become one with Excel. Now, put this book down and sit on it on the floor and chant… no, no, I'm joking. But organizing your thinking will help for what is ahead. Forget about how good you are with computers or numbers. In fact, I suck at math. When I look at Excel, especially the code behind it, called VBA I think in terms of sentence diagraming. Remember? In school when we had to diagram a sentence by nouns and verbs and such and draw lines out to the side. That is how my mind processes Excel; not as numbers and mathematics.

So, if you know some process very well, I want you to call upon that knowledge as we go forward. Make analogies in your mind to that process and compare it to the things I point out in this book. If you like football, think about that. Cooking? think of that. Whatever you need to help you and relax you.

I'm not going to get caught up on which version of Excel you have. I'm not going to explain which version is better and why I think so. There is Google if you need that. You bought this book because you wanted to finally wrap your mind around Excel and have that *ah-ha* moment. This is what chapter 1 is all about.

START HERE

Since I can't verbally ask you how much knowledge you have with Excel, I'm going to have to write this book so it's useful for everyone. Nothing is more annoying when reading a book like this and the first five chapters don't even apply to you. Maybe the writer will refund you for five chapters. So, I will start at a point that assumes not a basic knowledge with Excel but a basic experience with making a to-do list; like a grocery list. Whether you're seasoned with Excel or new to it, knowing how to build lists is important. After all, a spreadsheet is merely a list formatted as rows and columns or X-Y axis plots. Putting together those lists in a way that is expandable will help you as they grow.

Categorize everything! Group into groups. Typically, the category or group goes along the top of the spreadsheet and the lists of those groups on each row. This way it can be easily sorted, filtered, and counted.

Okay, but now that I said that, people often use Excel spreadsheets in different ways, so you may not want to structure your spreadsheet as a list of lists. You might want to use your spreadsheet as:

1. **A list of lists.**
2. **A form to be completed.**
3. **A calculator of figures/values.**
4. **A database of information.**

Or any other possibilities you can think. I've seen spreadsheets used like book manuscripts or even searchable Bible text programs. The abilities of Excel are very dynamic.

So, the first thing you need to do is decide how each of your "tabs" or sheets within the workbook are going to be used. Maybe one will do the first feature from the points above and another the second and so on. You could even hide some of the tabs and store supporting data there where the user won't be able to easily access and mess with it.

But one of the most powerful features of Excel is its ability to calculate and display data distinctively. Just storing numbers and words is one thing, but being able to not only add, subtract, multiply and do other mathematical equations but also identify and display things by changing colors and conditions is the real power behind Excel. You want to be able to automate some of the work you would normally do manually.

Excel's rich formula base allows you to do much of the heavy lifting. Once you learn how to write a formula in the way Excel expects (the *syntax*) then you can accomplish many amazing tasks.

CONCOCT A FORMULA

I often feel like a mad scientist when I write a real complex formula that does some amazing task that even I didn't think was possible. Sure, Excel can do A+B=X but it can also do things like count how many times B is in a list and if it is 43 times then turn a cell blue or if it is 56 times turn it green and on and on. You merely need to think of what you want to accomplish, and you can probably figure out how to write a formula to do it.

Excel even has a shortcut feature so you don't need to learn all the potential formula "functions" you can use. Just simply click on the function icon next to the formula bar and you get a list of formula functions you can use.

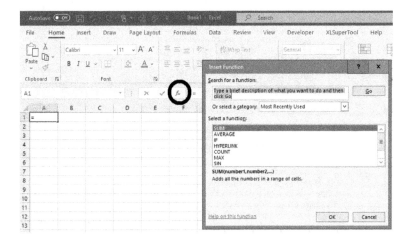

The formula functions are even categorized to help you figure out which one you might need.

Most of the time, people will use formulas from these 5 categories:

1. **Financial**
2. **Date & time**
3. **Math & Trig**
4. **Text**
5. **Logical**

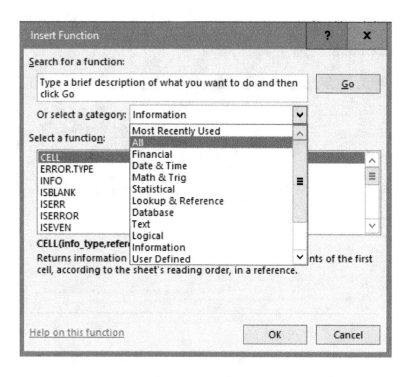

From these categories, you can do simple mathematical calculations or more complex conditional logic such as IF this is the result then do this other thing.

Think of these categories as your Excel toolbox. As I said earlier, associate this with some process you already do. If you are good at baking, this is your pots and pans, mixing spoons and such. If you are good at auto repair, this is your various wrenches and screwdrivers. Don't make it more complex than it is.

I learned Excel before understanding about the formula functions, so instead I often write them out longhand. This means instead of selecting from the formula bar, I type out the formula. You can do this by clicking into the formula bar or cell and typing an equal sign = then the formula you want. Some examples are:

- =2+2
- =sum(2+2)
- =A2+B2
- =sum(A2:B2)
- =if(sum(A2:B2)=4,"YES","NO")

Microsoft had the foresight to allow the user to accomplish the same task multiple ways rather than forcing you to use only one method. You can use "shortcuts" and "built-in" functions, or you can do it more manually as I demonstrated. Also, this is why I am not telling you every way you can accomplish something; just in case an advanced user is wondering why I haven't told the reader how to do something another way. Keep this in mind as you design more complex Excel spreadsheets. Try to anticipate that your user may do things multiple ways. If you don't plan to allow them to accomplish it, then at least inform them via comments or popup notes how to accomplish it your way.

WHAT'S ON THE MENU?

Another thing common with Microsoft products are menus and submenus. Many of the newer Microsoft products have visual menus rather than descriptive menus. This means, the menu element is a picture or an icon rather than a word you click on to do more things. Get to know where things are on the menu you are using. Again, I'm not going to assume which version of Excel you have, so look at your menu at the top of your Excel application and hover over the various elements to see what they do.

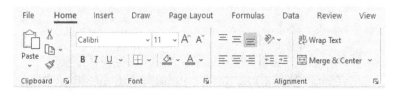

Most menus have a logical categorized structure. Think about what you are trying to do and go to that menu or submenu. Are you trying to change the margins? That is most likely under PAGE LAYOUT in the example. Do you want to do a spellcheck? That is most likely under the REVIEW menu. Think like you need to figure out which "drawer" you are keeping your socks as opposed to the drawer you keep your other clothing articles. It's simple if you think in organized thoughts. Don't let all the menus overwhelm you. **Process thinking!**

YOU SANK MY BATTLESHIP!

As mentioned earlier, inputting data into an Excel spreadsheet is like making a grocery list with categories of the aisles you will find the products. But perhaps a more detailed example of the Excel spreadsheet is like the old game Battleship. Remember how the players would secretly position their pieces on their side of the grid and you would take turns asking if you "hit" the piece by referencing its position on the grid? "A3, G22" and so on.

	A	B	C	D	E	F	G	H	I	J
1										
2										
3										
4			X							
5						X	X			
6		X						X		X
7				X						X
8	X	X						X		
9										
10										

Thinking like this will allow you to keep your mind organized once your spreadsheet becomes more complex. The concept is called an *axis*. More specifically, a 2D X-Y axis which simply means rows and columns that intersect at a point such as A3. The point where it intersects is called the *address* or more specifically since we are dealing with blocks or cells, it is the cell address. A group of cells are called a *range*.

As you add formulas to your spreadsheet, you'll refer to cell and range addresses. You will tell your formula to do various things based on these cells and ranges.

The key is to know where you are on your spreadsheet. When you click into a cell or range, Excel borders the cells. You can also know where you are by looking at the *Name Box* at the top left edge of the spreadsheet where the selected top left most cell address is displayed.

Process thinking gets you to think more about the process than the details. We often stumble over details which can make the process more difficult. However, if you get too far into a big-picture process and have not considered the details, you may also experience process failures. Imagine building a car and not considering it may experience a flat tire at some point so you will need a place to put the spare tire. This could be a critical design flaw in the process.

So, as you think about what you want your spreadsheet and workbook to do, think about its expandability. Where are you going to store that "spare tire" and hey, the jack that you'll need. Or maybe your project isn't going to be that complex. Maybe all you're going to do with the spreadsheet is make a grocery list that doesn't require any mathematical formulas or complicated cell references.

No matter how you plan to use Excel, thinking in a process way will put you leaps and bounds ahead of people who think Excel is just a bunch of little boxes into which to shove things.

CHAPTER 2 ORGANIZED MIND

The running joke is that a messy desk is the sign of an organized mind, but I'm not so certain that is true. In a society that worries about people with OCD (obsessive compulsive disorder) and ADHD (attention deficit hyperactivity disorder) we might want to reconsider how to organize our minds. Yeah, this book isn't just going to help you with spreadsheets; haha – anyhow, you are going to learn a lot of tricks about Excel and I'm sorry, but you just aren't going to remember it all. You need a way to store this information in a place other than just your mind.

NOTEPAD

I like to use Windows Notepad to store all the little tricks and formula snippets I learned over the years. I guess if you're an Apple user, TextEdit is the comparable program to Notepad. You might think, why not put all these things into a spreadsheet where you can filter and categorize and do all the fancy stuff for which Excel was made? I tried that but I found I needed to just quickly put them somewhere, plus Excel wanted to execute my formula snippets even if they weren't referring to real cell addresses. It just seems better to have a note of things. Believe me, you will catch yourself asking, *"How did I do XYZ?"* You will want to recall how you did something you did six months ago.

Don't try to save everything in one long notepad file. You will not want to sift through all of that. It's better to save them in a single folder but as individual snippet files. Then name them something descriptive enough that you know what they are before you open them. In this way, you can also quickly send friends and workmates the snippet. Wow, you're a hero!

Also, I found – and this is going to sound strange coming from the author of a self-help book – but that you will rarely consult a book on Excel while you are in the midst of using Excel. Exactly the reason I hope you are reading this book BEFORE you open that spreadsheet. You've seen it; people have 3-4 books wedged in between their monitor and the wall but the books are from 1987. The version of software those books are about aren't even in use anymore. Clear out the clutter. It's the 21st century after all. We are supposed to be slaves to killer robots or aliens or something. Keep your own reference materials. You can do it. You are your own best teacher.

TEN MILLION TABS

Depending how you are using your spreadsheet, you may want or need to use multiple tabs, but keep in mind that like anything, the more parts the more complex. Industries from manufacturing to the IRS (haha) have a principle of K.I.S.S. *"keep it simple, stupid"*. Complexity for complication's sake is, well…stupid. Having a little data on one tab and more on another and another and another is often stupid and unnecessary. Why can't you have 2 tabs; source and display or interface?

Suppose you have a spreadsheet of ice cream flavors, costs and profit margin. Yes, I know; what sinister maniac is making money off the sweet, cold goodness that is ice cream? But anyhow, you could have multiple tabs separated by flavors or prices and another one with the profit margins, selling locations and on and on. Now you will need to click on the different tabs to see the various information.

What if instead you kept all the data on one tab and had another tab where you could select the various elements you want to see? This way the data is all in one place and there is no need to go looking for it. Sure, you could use a workbook wide search and I'll tell you how to do it.

Press CTRL+F then the search box will popup

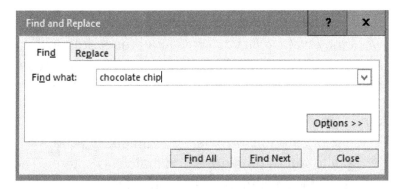

Select the Options >> box and have it search Within: workbook. This will search for chocolate chip on EVERY tab. Still a clunky way to do it. You need to start thinking like a machine, like a computer before they outsource your job to a machine…okay, not funny.

Organizing, or re-organizing our minds to think more like a Google analytic will not only help us design better Excel workbooks but allow us to participate in the data-driven world we now live.

Once you figure out how to structure your data on one tab, you can create another tab that interacts with and displays the data in a way the user needs to see it. Just like having ten million tabs, many people don't like to look at ten million columns and rows of data. You are going to serve it up for them so that they don't have to go dumpster diving for data.

A HUMAN'S CHOICE

Now you will need to decide how the user will tell you what they want. Will you provide a preset dropdown box of choices or will you allow them to free-text type into a cell and off you go to return their selection?

Since your data is on the other SOURCE tab, as a long list of categorized lists, you can easily write a formula to return data based on matching criteria. The user might be asked to give criteria like:

1. **FLAVOR**
2. **PRICE**

You could accomplish this with a LOOKUP & REFERENCE formula from our formula functions list. A lot of people like to use the HLOOKUP and VLOOKUP formulas, which means horizontal and vertical lookup – by row or column.

I don't care for HLOOKUP or VLOOKUP; too much thinking about which row or column I'm in. Instead I use two functions called INDEX and MATCH.

> **=index(range to return, match(criteria, range to match,0))**

Shhh, this is my most powerful secret. Don't tell anyone.

Using index and match, I can tell my formula to look in the range of flavors and return the price of the flavor I desired.

TAB1 or SHEET1 – the interface/display tab

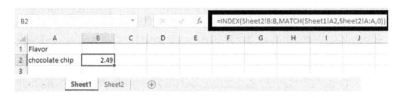

Cell B2 contains the index-match formula which references cell A2 and ranges on Sheet2 so that it returns the price based on the user's input into cell A2.

Let's look what the data source tab looks like.

TAB2 or SHEET2 – the data source tab

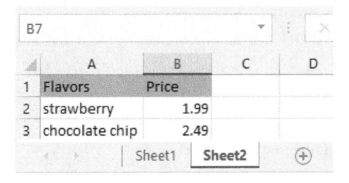

As you see, it merely contains the list of flavors and prices. Range or column A and range B.

Now back to our formula that we wrote on tab1.

=index(range to return, match(criteria, range to match,0))

The above formula won't actually work. It is just the syntax or explanation of what is needed to write the formula. You need to tell the index what range to look into (range A of tab2) and then what criteria to look for and in what range on tab2. The zero at the end simply means only return exact matches. This is more for when doing number or value matches, not the text lookup we're doing in the example.

=index(**Sheet2!B:B,** match(**Sheet1!A2, Sheet2!A:A,0**))

A lot of programming works kind of backwards because it "wraps" the desired final result at the beginning of the formula. In this case, we logically might think we want to write the formula as match X against Y and return (index) Z. Here the result is expressed first. It is as if we are asking the question in reverse.

"Tell me the result of matching X against Y"

We don't know Z, that's what we're trying to get. Damned Algebra!!!!

Also, we could tell it to only look in a specific range A1:A20, but why limit ourselves at this stage?

22

That was just one example of how to use a tab as the display or interface tab. Our example required the user to type in criteria into cell A2 of tab1. But what if we wanted to have the user select from a dropdown list?

First, click into cell A2 of tab1, delete the text already there. Remember the menus? Find the DATA menu and look for or search for DATA VALIDATION. A popup box will appear like this:

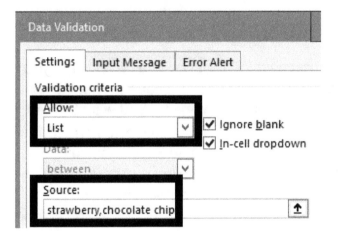

Select List from the Allow box and type in comma separated choices in the Source box. The choices are the selections of ice cream flavors in this example.

If you did everything correctly you will now have a way to select from a dropdown box in cell A2 of tab1.

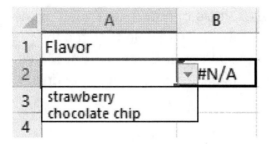

There are more advanced ways to set up these selection choices but that is beyond the scope of this chapter and this book. So much for a choice eh?

ONLINE REFERENCES

Now that you paid for this book and you're all the way into chapter 2, I guess I can tell you this, but the Internet has everything you need. You want to learn how to build a garage out of Lego blocks? Got it! You want to learn how to better use Excel, got that too. But these websites may not always exist, nor do they come with my sense of humor. So, aren't you glad you bought this book? Here's a few to get you started:

- https://support.office.com/en-us/excel
- https://www.mrexcel.com/
- https://www.excel-easy.com/
- https://www.exceltip.com/

Try out the forums where you can ask questions to specific issues. A live "expert" will answer.

CHAPTER 3 FALSE START FRUSTRATIONS

Before you design that masterpiece spreadsheet that will finally get you carried aloft through the office on your workmates shoulders, you should consider that it is most likely they will give you just enough Excel rope to hang yourself; they won't give you enough information to properly design the spreadsheet. They will forget this and that crucial element even after you asked them five times before you formatted the workbook in a way that would require a lot of rework if they left anything out.

So, let's practice asking the questions that hopefully help save you frustrating false starts.

First, we need to consider what kind of workbook is needed:

1. **A list of lists.**
2. **A form to be completed.**
3. **A calculator of figures/values.**
4. **A database of information.**

Will it need formulas? How many people will be accessing it? Where will it be stored; on a single computer or on the network?

WHAT IS WANTED VS NEEDED

As you interact with your Excel project "customer", try to determine from them what is wanted versus what is needed. Make them realize that while almost anything is "possible" to create in the spreadsheet, the issue is how much time and effort will be invested.

Plan a meeting with the customer and if possible, use a big screen to discuss the project. It would be good if you could use a spreadsheet to take and organize the notes from the meeting. This will help the customer think in Excel terms. You can even use the handy move feature.

Select the range by holding your left mouse button and dragging the range to another place on the spreadsheet. Many non-Excel users find this simple process amazing. Hey, hey it's magic!

	A	B	C	D	E
1	1. Note blah blah blah				
2	2. Note blah blah blah				
3	3. Note blah blah blah				
4	4. Note bla ah blah				
5	5. Note blah blah blah				

Just consider that no matter how many questions you ask them in developing their project, they will almost always come back with more requests. However, take this as a good thing, as it may just mean you have them now thinking of all the possibilities Excel can accomplish. This is why you should always make your project expandable and as generic as possible.

BY THE NUMBERS

Next, do yourself a favor and have your customer tell you exactly what mathematical equations are needed in the project. In this way, if something goes wrong, it was their own error. I'm not trying to get you to pass the buck or "cover your ass" so much as I am trying to get you to simply put the responsibility back onto the customer. This will save you a world of hurt when in some future scenario, the calculations go awry.

The customer need not be able to write a formula to give you the equation, but they should be able to write it out for you in a way you can "translate" into a formula. You should probably run a few examples by them before you commit it to the actual project.

If you're like me, you aren't Einstein's illegitimate great, great grandchild so numbers aren't really your thing. But fortunately, Excel has enough mathematical functions to handle just about anything your customer may send your way.

Basic mathematical operators between numbers are written like this:

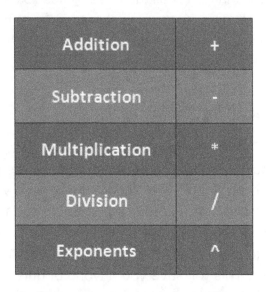

Addition	+
Subtraction	-
Multiplication	*
Division	/
Exponents	^

After these basic operators, you'll need to consider what is called "order of operation". This is where it is important to place parentheses in the correct part of the formula.

- =2*4+2
- =2*(4+2)
- =(2*4+2)

Results are different based on their order of operation.

While basic order of operation isn't too complex, it gets trickier as you need to make the formula longer. It is a good idea to try out the segments of the formula before putting it all together. In our previous example:

=2*4+2 is 2x4 then add 2, resulting in 10

Whereas

=2*(4+2) is 2x6, resulting in 12

Whereas

=(2*4+2) is still 2x4 then add 2, resulting in 10

Now imagine doing something more complex like

=2*(4+2)/4*(8-5)

Add to that, you most likely won't be referring to static numbers but rather cell references. Your formula might end up looking more like this:

=A2*(G15+R8)/X2*(Z1-G16)

Now you must follow the flow or logic of the references. Hopefully, no one wipes out the formula in those cells. We'll talk about locking or protecting the sheet later. Don't become overwhelmed. Just organize your mind and associate this organization concept with processes you already know how to do well.

KNOW YOUR LIMITS

As you begin to work with Excel or even if you are a pro, you should consider limits like the maximum number of characters that can be typed in an individual cell or maximum rows on a sheet. This varies with different versions of Excel, so you'll want to look up your version. Here is a URL shortened link to the Microsoft support page on these specs.

shorturl.at/eijPT

But when thinking of limits, it's not just what Excel can and can't do; because as I said previously Excel can do a helluva whole lot. We haven't even discussed the VBA capabilities of Excel yet. The limitations I'm talking about are the limitations of your own knowledge combined with your time and effort. Your customer will keep coming back to you to reengineer something you did two years ago. Will you even remember how your own creation works? I know I often don't. I almost invariably must relearn what I did in the first place.

This is also why it is important to:

1. **Keep a notepad of snippets.**
2. **Design expandable and generic.**
3. **Be consistent.**
4. **Add instructional comments, especially to Macro modules.**

Being consistent for me is as simple as using the same cell colorization to indicate all the same things on my worksheets. For me it is:

- **YELLOW** = dropdown selection
- **GREEN** = input needed
- **GRAY** = formula in cell (usually protected)
- **RED** = alert or warning

Having said that, I've worked on projects where the customer wanted it their way and I conformed even when it made little sense. Sometimes you will have to adapt. Don't be a pompous jerk. It's an Excel spreadsheet, not a Rembrandt.

All of these suggestions will help you avoid false starts. But even more, you may need to sometimes say no. If a customer keeps having you design and redesign an Excel project, it is most likely because they don't know exactly what they want. It may be necessary to have them organize their own thoughts before they have you launching on their wild rabbit hunts. I've even designed submission forms, in Excel so that the customer will present their ideas in a way that is conducive to becoming a project. It has the two-fold effect of getting them to think within a set of parameters and letting you demonstrate your Excel prowess.

I feel like I need a screenshot or something here. Here's one for you. Go take a coffee or tea break and come back okay?

CHAPTER 4 TALKING EXCEL

Every industry or group has its own "language"; whether we're talking about making cupcakes or launching rockets, these endeavors develop a way of speaking or talking about their subject matter. Even your place of work may have its own unique terms that make no sense outside the workplace. Excel has its own language and way of expressing. Here we will be talking about learning the language of Excel.

In the previous chapter I used a cell reference and wrote it as Z1 but how is this different than writing it as Z1?

Placing the dollar sign before the column tells Excel to keep the reference as Z even if you drag the formula to another column. In the same way, putting a dollar sign before the row, indicates that you want the row number to remain static even if the formula is dragged down.

- **$Z1** = keep column static.
- **Z$1** = keep row static.
- **Z1** = keep column and row static.
- **Z1** = allow column and row to change as dragged to next column or row.

But talking Excel, or like an Excel expert requires more than just knowing how to properly write a formula so it will execute correctly. Like your industry or workplace, you'll need to learn terms. These are only a few terms. I hope I have captured the most common.

1. **Address** = range or cell number, column and row
2. **Calculation** = Excel updating formula calculations
3. **Cell** = single position/block on worksheet
4. **Clipboard** = copied data using CTRL+C
5. **Code** = generically, a formula or Macro/VBA module
6. **Condition** = in a formula, a IF X then Y statement
7. **Conditional Formatting** = changing cell based on some condition or result
8. **Developer** = hidden by default menu to VBA editor
9. **Editor** = VBA/Module editor
10. **Filter** = ordering rows by some condition
11. **Format** = style of cell, text, number, color
12. **Formula** = code executed on worksheet, not VBA
13. **Function** = word/syntax to execute within formula

14. **Height** = cell or page height typically
15. **Macro** = VBA code, module or shortcut key
16. **Menu** = text or icon/picture-based options
17. **Merge** = combine multiple cells into one
18. **Module** = VBA code
19. **Named Range** = aliasing a cell or range by a name
20. **Quick Access Toolbar (QAT)** = User-defined menu
21. **Range** = one or multiple cells, their address
22. **Reference** = address of range
23. **Ribbon** = icon/picture menu at top of Excel
24. **Sheet/Tab** = individual tab within workbook
25. **Sort** = ordering sequentially or alphabetically
26. **Sum** = total of a range
27. **Text type/Number type** = style or format of a cell
28. **Toolbar** = typically quick options above and below Excel application
29. **Userform** = VBA popup box, usually user created
30. **Value** = number, not text
31. **Width** = cell or page width
32. **Workbook** = an individual Excel file
33. **Worksheet** = a tab within a workbook
34. **Wrap** = force cell to wrap around to see entire text

Once you understand these few terms, you can go to any Excel conference and sound cool while sipping a latte with your fellow Excel nerds...or at least you'll be able to better interact with other Excel users. For example, many people wrongly use the words Sort and Filter. In Excel, a Filter could be almost any indicated sequence. A Sort is usually either numeric or alphabetic. A Filter typically only shows the filtered criteria whereas the sort will show all data but sorted.

Applying a filter to your data list is as easy as selecting the row where the categories or title are then select DATA menu and click on the Filter funnel. Then you can filter by any column(s).

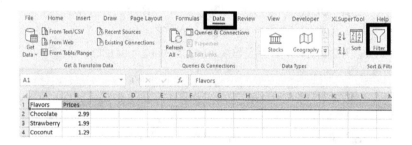

There are more advanced ways to apply filters and sorting, but this should get you pointed in the right direction and get you to understand the difference.

SPRINGS & SPROCKETS

Behind the curtain or under the hood of Excel is something even more powerful. Shhhh, don't tell anyone. This is going to be the thing that separates you from that pencil-protector dude in the next cubicle. The engine behind it all is a thing called VBA or Visual Basic for Applications. This is the "computer language" used by most of the Microsoft Applications such as Word, Powerpoint, Access and yes Excel.

When you learn how to tap into VBA and write code segments (modules/macros) in Excel you can do things other Excel users can barely imagine. You could do things like:

- Hide or reveal a sheet based on some condition.

- Compare multiple workbooks and sheets to each other by having the macro open them in the background.

- Email workbooks/sheets to people.

If you have never used VBA before, don't become intimidated before we even start. Remember, Process thinking! Organized Mind! You can do this.

The first thing you'll need to do if you haven't already is to activate the Developer Menu (or Tab). Typically, you can do this by going to FILE/OPTIONS/CUSTOM RIBBONS while in any workbook. It will activate it for all future sessions of Excel you open so you won't need to repeat this step.

Look for the word "Developer" and check the box next to it. Remember, this may not be the same in all versions of Excel. You may need to Google it if you can't find it.

Customize the Ribbon: ⓘ

Main Tabs	▼

Main Tabs
- ⊞ ✔ Background Removal
- ⊞ ✔ **Home**
- ⊞ ✔ Insert
- ⊞ ✔ Draw
- ⊞ ✔ Page Layout
- ⊞ ✔ Formulas
- ⊞ ✔ Data
- ⊞ ✔ Review
- ⊞ ✔ View
- ⊞ ✔ Developer
- ✔ Add-ins

I mentioned looking it up on Google. We should actually practice using search engines because there is no way you're going to remember everything even if you become an Excel expert, since an expert is merely an amateur with a lot of practice.

When looking up information, don't type out a sentence like: *How do I find the developer menu in Excel?* Rather use key words like this:

developer menu excel activate

While search engines try to be human friendly and "guess" at what you're trying to ask, it could also look for the extraneous words you don't really need, like "how do I find" instead of just "developer menu excel". You'll get cleaner results if you are concise.

You don't need to worry about capitalizing words. It will still find it. If you want to only search for specific words then put quotes around your phrase, like:

"developer menu"

Using a search engine is going to help you out when you have written that killer formula or code or that VBA macro that just needs one more little piece to make it work properly. Also, consult the references I mentioned in chapter 2. **Process Thinking! Organized Mind!**

Enter the Editor

If everything worked activating the Developer Menu, you should now see a new menu option at the top of every Excel session you open.

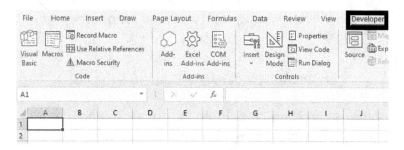

When you click on Developer it will open the Developer options which should include things like Visual Basic and Macros.

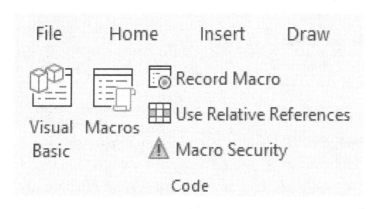

Don't worry, you haven't just accessed some secret backdoor to Microsoft. It is part of Excel and designed to allow you more control over Excel. Cool eh?

Just in case the workbook you're in already has VBA code in it, let's look at a fresh workbook. Make sure all other workbooks are closed and then open a blank, new workbook. Click on the Developer Menu then the Visual Basic option.

You should now see something like this:

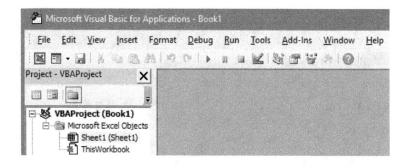

This is the VBA editor. From here you can create modules/macros and popup forms with all kinds of buttons, boxes, and other controls. No more simple =A1+B1 here. You are going to be amazing!

Let's write our first module/macro...or you can go to the bathroom. Don't worry. I'll be right here when you come back. Alrighty then, let's start.

While inside the VBA editor, click on INSERT then select Module from the dropdown box.

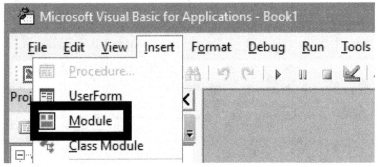

You should now see a huge white blank box. This is your canvas. It is in here we are going to type our first macro.

Each macro/module is actually a larger part of the thing we're going to do which is actually called a *subroutine*. Stick with me here. Maybe think of it like this:

- **Excel Application** = the Body
- **Workbook** = the Head
- **Worksheets** = the Limbs
- **Formula** = the Actions, expressions
- **VBA** = the Mind
- **Module** = a collection of thoughts
- **Subroutine** = a single thought

So we're going to add a new single thought.

Click into the white blank box and type the following. Capitalization doesn't matter at this time.

HINT: If you type **sub newthought** and press the ENTER key, the editor will automatically put the brackets () and the End Sub in there. Then all you need is the two lines inbetween.

```
(General)

    Sub newthought()
    Sheet1.Range("a1") = "this is a new thought."
    Sheet1.Range("a1").Interior.Color = vbGreen
    End Sub
```

You have now written a subroutine which sometimes people wrongly call a module or macro. Next we want to run it. If you did everything correctly you can press the PLAY/RUN button at the top of the VBA editor.

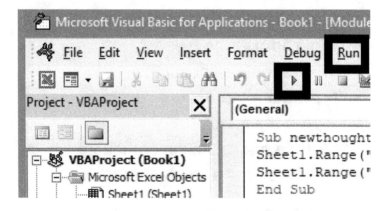

Now go the the workbook, sheet1 and see your result. Did it work? If not, go back and try again. Type everything exactly. You need the quotation marks everywhere I show.

Imagine writing more detailed and useful subroutines that "call" on each other and do amazing things. But first, you need to understand what you wrote.

Sub newthought ()

This is the name of the subroutine and should always be without spaces and descriptive enough to help you know at a glance what it's supposed to do. The brackets are for *arguments* of the subroutine. We'll get into that later but an argument might be something you want the subroutine to act upon like a string of text or a value.

Sheet1.Range("a1")

Is simply a reference to sheet or tab 1 and the range/cell A1.

.Interior.Color = vbGreen

Is a property of the range/cell which we can change through VBA. Here we turn the interior color green. Excel has a few shortcut default colors.

End Sub

Simply, the end of the subroutine.

If everything worked properly, then on sheet1 you should see text in cell A1 and the cell should be green.

Now stop here for a moment. If you are thinking like an Excel Guru, you should be thinking, *"Damn! I could do all kinds of shhtuff with this VBA junk!"* Yes, yes you can and that's exactly what I want you to do.

So, the next few chapters are going to speed up our process thinking and get us thinking more like an Excel Guru. In no time, you will be the nerdiest person at the party, eh nevermind. Stop reading for a moment. Put this book away and open a blank spreadsheet and try out some of the stuff we've discussed. Or if you are already more advanced, go do all kinds of amazing things and curse my name as a dumb newbie. How dare I write a book. Hahaha. Either way, get your mind pumping out Excel magic then come back and start the next chapter.

CHAPTER 5 COME TOGETHER

Why can't I use one of my favorite Beatles songs as a title of a chapter of my book? But this chapter is about more than bushy haired bugs with guitars, it's about putting your formula and VBA experiences together.

Don't worry, if you are like; "*But I don't even know what I'm doing yet!*" This chapter, hopefully like all the previous chapters should be of interest even to "experts" and newbies alike, even if the experts are just cussing me right now for not telling you about their favorite Excel feature.

First let me ask you something. Just between you and me. And be honest okay? Did you even look at any of the reference websites I gave you in chapter 2? If you did, then you are probably already writing more complex formulas and subroutines because you are either trying out things you saw at those websites or what I've said so far is clicking and you are eager to move forward.

One problem I experince and perhaps you will too, is when to use a sheet formula and when to write a subroutine. Here are a few questions to ask yourself before you crack open the VBA editor and go to town.

1. **Is it worth the trouble?**
2. **What problems will it cause?**

Not just worth the trouble and time you may put into writing a subroutine but worth the trouble explaining how to use it compared to a simple formula.

What problems it could cause is that the enduser won't know how or does not have permissions to run macros so the subroutine approach won't work for them.

Beyond that, consider why it is important to write a subroutine rather than just make a formula. I've used subroutines because I'm not allowed to protect a sheet but I need to make sure the data is persistent. My subroutine can make sure no one deletes important data; it will simply repopulate the cells if they do.

Conditional Statements

As a matter of fact, this is a perfect time to talk about conditional statements. Sometimes people call them IF THEN statements. If you are Process Thinking and using an Organized Mind, you should have started thinking like an Excel programmer, not only while writing formula and VBA code but in your everyday life. You are beginning to see information as data to process. Is it true? If so do this with it, if not do that with it.

In a sheet formula, the syntax or proper structure to write a conditional statement is:

=IF(logical-test, result-if-true, result-if-false)

Example:

=IF(2+2=4,"Yes","No")

You could substitutle the 2+2=4 with many things such as comparing two cells

=IF(A1=B1, "Yes","No")

And the Yes and No could be substituted with any result you want. Just remember the first is true/positive and the second argument is false/negative.

=IF(A1=B1, 42,666)

The VBA subroutine version of a conditional
statement looks like this:

```
Sub conditstatement ()
If 2 + 2 = 4 Then
conditionalresult = "yes"
Else
conditionalresult = "no"
End If
MsgBox conditionalresult
End Sub
```

There are simpler ways to write this subroutine but
this example is in a form that helps you understand
what is happening. Remember, you can name your
subroutine almost anything you want without spaces
so I named the example **conditstatement**.

We then create a variable (like a alias for the result) to
become the true or false result. I used
conditionalresult. You could call it whatever you
want.

Lastly, the **MsgBox** is simply telling Excel to show the
result as a popup box. Try it out! Do you remember
how to get to the VBA Editor?

HINT: Developer Menu, Visual Basic, Insert Module.

Another form of a conditional statement is Conditional Formatting which changes the look of the cell(s) depending on the result in the cell(s). Typically, you may want to change the color of the cells to indicate a favorable or unfavorable result; such as red or green.

This can be accomplished with the Conditional Formatting feature usually found within the HOME menu.

Conditional
Formatting ˇ

With this feature, you write conditions for the selected cells or an entire column or range. There are some default conditions you can select. Some examples are:

- **Highlight if greater or less than**
- **Highlight if equal to**
- **Highlight if contains text**
- **Highlight duplicates**

You could use the Color Scales feature to shade the cells depending how much they are towards a top and bottom number. Or you could even write your own formula instead of using the defaults. Just remember, the "IF" part is implied in Conditional Formatting.

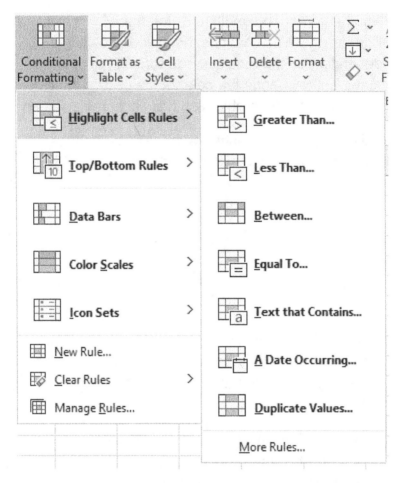

So, learning to write Excel formulas and Excel VBA code is like learning how to write in a foreign language and then how to write a technical manual in that foreign language. While the task may at first seem daunting, you'll begin to see how these processes come together and even compliment and aid each other.

Bringing it all together in Excel is when you finally find yourself writing sheet formulas inside a VBA environment. What I mean by this, is that sometimes you will know how to do something as a formula but not know how to do it in a VBA module, so you simply use the formula inside the module. Something like this:

As a sheet formula

> =match("red", A:A, 0)

That formula will look at column A and return the row number of the first time it finds the word "red".

As a VBA code

> redfound = application.match("red", sheet1.range("A:A"),0)

Of course, as I've said before, there are always different ways to accomplish the same thing in Excel and Microsoft products in general.

You could write the VBA code this way

> redfound = Range("A:A").Find("red").Row

All of these examples return the row where the first instance of the word *red* is found in column A. After you know what row it is on, you could go on to do other things with it.

The key here is that you are switching your mind back and forth between Excel formula and Excel VBA; sort of like how you may speak more casually among friends but more professionally in a work meeting. This ability will help you in your Excel world.

Ask the Experts

Remember those Excel websites/forums I told you about in Chapter 2? Did you visit any of them yet? What would be a good practice is to go sign up for an account (which is usually free) and go to the message board or forums part of the website. Find the place you are allowed to ask questions and ask how to write the VBA version of something you already know how to do in a formula. Then go try it out in the Developer VBA Editor.

I keep urging you to do this and if you do, I run the risk of you not finishing reading this book. You might find out that you don't need me because you "*ain't no dummy*". Oh, well. That's a good thing!

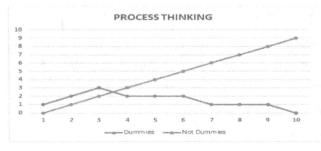

Introducing Pivot Tables

Putting it all together will require understanding pivot tables and charts as well. Yes, yes I know. This is the part many people hate. What the heck is a pivot table anyhow? Think of it as a summary of the data but in a way that the user can easily look at different parts.

If you had a list of favorite ice cream flavors and how many cartons you had of each in the freezer, and perhaps on which days you plan on eating which flavor before its expiration date; a pivot table could easily count up those numbers and display them in a more readable way. Pivot tables also will allow you to make cool charts!

	A	B	C
1	Flavor	cartons	expiration
2	vanilla	1	3/10/2110
3	chocolate	1	2/16/2110
4	rockyroad	1	4/11/2110
5	strawberry	1	2/16/2110
6	vanilla	1	4/12/2110
7	chocolate	1	3/11/2110
8	rockyroad	1	1/1/2110
9	strawberry	1	2/11/2109

Then when we select all the data and INSERT/PIVOT TABLE we can begin to see the data in a more summarized or "aggregated" way…without being aggravated.

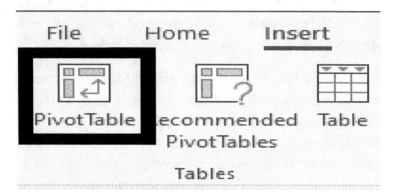

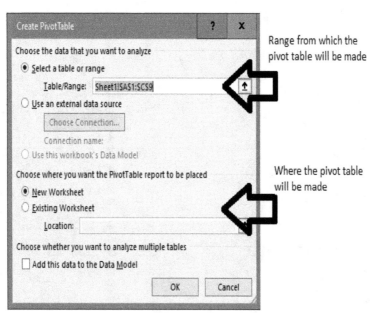

Range from which the pivot table will be made

Where the pivot table will be made

Here comes the tricky part for most new users, setting up the pivot table element. But don't let it be tricky. Process thinking. It is simply organizing pieces you want.

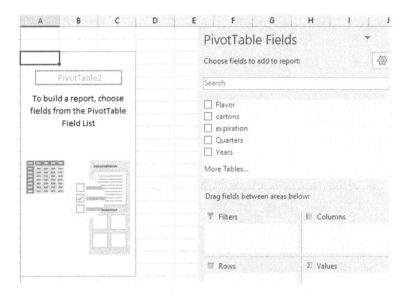

The empty pivot table is shown on the left and the "field list" of elements you can select is shown on the right. The elements are your headers from your data.

For a basic pivot table, you might want to see the flavors show in rows and the "values" (anything that can be counted) of the cartons in the Values field. You might want to see the expiration dates in the Columns field.

Click on the elements in the field list to the right, hold down the left mouse button and drag to fields below.

When you're all done, your pivot table might look like this:

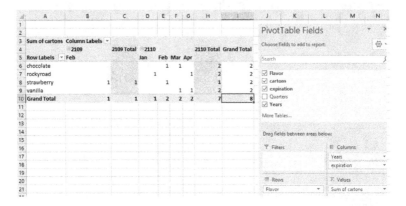

To some degree, there is no right or wrong way to set up a pivot table except for how the user wants to see the data displayed. You might put your flavors in the Columns field and the expiration in the Rows field. Go ahead and try it. Drag the elements in the field list out of the current fields and into the other fields. You won't break it. I say that with the exception to make sure you realize whether you are counting or summing a value. Note how it says SUM OF CARTONS. You could also make the pivot table count the cartons. You could change the numbering format to show decimal places or currency and all sorts of ways to show the data.

Introducing Charts

You can make charts without having a pivot table if your data list is simple enough but since pivot tables summarize your data, you can tie charts to that summary and have the chart change when the data changes. But adding charts to a pivot table and getting the chart to show what you want it to show may limit how the pivot table is structured. It may require you putting flavors in Columns versus Rows for example. Again, you'll have to play around with the structure until you get it how you like. You can't break it.

To INSERT a basic bar chart, we restructured the pivot table. Yours will be color!

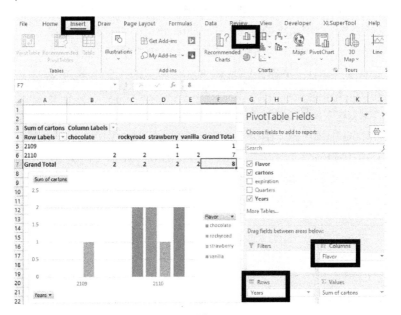

Just like with pivot tables, you can move the data around or use different types of charts to show your information. The key is, you have the flexibility to move things around. For me to tell you step-by-step what to do makes you a robot, not a guru. Go try out adding charts!

This chapter was about putting all your new skills together. Eventually, as you get more creative you might RECORD MACRO as you make a pivot table or a chart and then assign that macro to a button you can press that easily makes the chart or pivot table. Yeah, you'll be doing those kinds of things if you aren't already.

This book isn't like other Excel books that will bore you to death with step-by-step examples that don't help you adapt to your specific issue or business. Instead, I mean for this book to help you think like an Excel guru. I want you to exceed this book in a short time. Maybe write your own book. But for now, why not take a break before the next chapter. Go get some fresh air, make a sandwich, or smoke…shhhh, I'm not supposed to write that in a book. Enjoy! I'll be here when you get back.

CHAPTER 6 TOOLS & TRICKS

Since this book isn't like all the other Excel books you've read or might read, it is here where I want to encourage you to think differently. Many self-help books give you just enough information to string you along. They want you to buy future editions. I have no plans to write another Excel book, so I have one shot to help pass on my tools and tricks of the trade. My decades of Excel experience are coming to an end as I transition out of being an Excel guru and passing the torch to you.

Anything is Possible

I have spent years helping people who begin their requests with asking; "*Is it possible to..?*" Of course, anything is possible. It is just a matter if it can be figured out and how much time and effort someone wants to invest. People stopped asking me if something was possible and THAT is when I became a guru. That is when you too will become a guru.

But first, like every good wizard, you'll need a bag of spells and tricks and magic potions; or at least as an Excel guru you need a place to keep all your code snippets. As I suggested before, you should have a place on your computer that you keep all of these.

Sure, you could write them in a notebook but then you'd be unable to quickly copy and paste them into your spreadsheet or your VBA editor.

Like a retiring magician, I'd like to share some of my "secret" tricks with you. Shhhh, don't tell anyone.

Formulas

Knowing how to handwrite a formula, rather than just using the INSERT FUNCTION feature, is a powerful way to not only ingrain a formula into your mind but it helps you to think like Excel. So, I would suggest that even if you prefer to press the insert function icon, you should sometimes type it out.

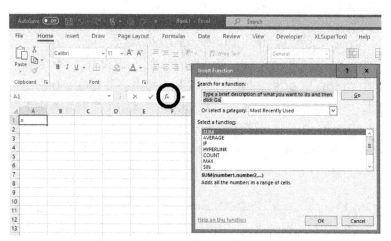

Start building a list of formulas that help you quickly achieve a common request. One such formula is the

MATCH formula. People always want to see if one item in a column is in another column (or range).

As you build your list of special Excel formulas, be careful not to use formulas that are only available in later versions of Excel. There is nothing worse than sending a client a killer spreadsheet and all the formulas fail because they only have the older version. Also, be cognizant of how the user might manipulate your formulas and break them. For example, do you need to make the reference static with the $ such as A1 rather than A1 in case the user drags down your formula?

Understanding how your formulas are going to be used will help you write them in a way that kind of dummy-proofs them. I often put TRIM around formulas I know are supposed to be returning text or a string.

=trim(a5)

In this way, I try to predict the user accidentally putting spaces at the beginning or end of text, which could cause trouble with matching, sorting, and filtering.

If you start thinking like this, you will become an Excel guru.

Macros & Subroutines

In the same way you build a list of useful formulas, you should build a toolset of macros or subroutines. For me, one of the most useful is the one that disables and enables all the things that slow a subroutine down.

```
'optimize macro by disabling all processes that slow it down.

Application.ScreenUpdating = False

Application.Calculation = xlCalculationManual

Application.EnableEvents = False

Application.DisplayAlerts = False
```

But then to re-enable you would need something like this at the end of the subroutine.

```
'Re-enable screenupdating (before END SUB)

Application.ScreenUpdating = True

Application.Calculation = xlCalculationAutomatic

Application.EnableEvents = True

Application.DisplayAlerts = True

Application.StatusBar = False
```

You could make some user-defined functions (UDF) to use instead but often a "coder" (that's you) will forget that the enduser doesn't have the UDF and the subroutine will fail. So, I find it best to try to add the code snippets right into the workbook. Psst? Did you look up Excel and user-defined functions? If you don't know what I'm talking about you really should Google it. Remember, this book isn't about explaining every little detail to the point you forget it from page to page, but rather it's about helping you think like an Excel guru.

Now, if you are thinking like an Excel guru and you look back at my two macros to optimize and re-enable a subroutine, you should, to some degree understand what each does. You didn't just gloss over my code, did you?

I often will place the "re-enable" script at the start of a subroutine as well in case a spreadsheet had various application functions turned off before my subroutine was ran. How's that possible you might ask?

Imagine the user has several workbooks open and one of the workbooks has code by someone else. Suppose the code is poorly written and has disabled various application processes. This might cause a problem for your code or calculations. Always assume that you have to start fresh. Always assume someone or something has already sabotaged you. Sometimes being paranoid is a good thing. This way, your code runs smoothly and maybe fixes issues the user didn't even know they had. You're a guru!

Always Over Engineer

Another thing to being an Excel guru is anticipating your customer's next request before they even voice it. Build into your projects a way to expand or modify it without too much reworking. Make your projects generic enough that you could easily use it for other things. This way you merely need to modify it a little and you're done.

But what you should especially do is always over engineer. Build the project with failure in mind. For example, I had an enduser that I developed what I thought was the perfect solution for her dilemma, but she kept reporting that it wasn't working for her. I tested and tested, and it worked fine for me. Eventually, I sat right next to her as she used my Excel tool and what she did was obviously the problem. She would enter a number and press the spacebar then the enter key. What this did is turn the value/number into a string and so Excel wasn't calculating it correctly. So, from now on, on every project, I assume someone will do the same thing. I wrap my formulas into a TRIM or VALUE when I want to force it to be a number.

=TRIM(A2)

=VALUE(A2)

I also do so in subroutines. Again, assume your project is going to be abused and misused.

Be careful telling people how much you have over engineered your project, since they could say it isn't necessary. You're an artist. Who are they to tell you how to paint your master pieces? I had one fellow claim that all the extra stuff I added was "cutesy" stuff, as if I was merely adding fluff. His problem was that he was using Excel as a word processing program with a calculator on the side rather than as a ledger program with powerful cross-referencing abilities. He didn't need a guru. No reason to pull rabbits out of hats if all the people want is to eat carrots…or something like that.

Give Away Your Secrets

One of the reasons I wrote this book, besides hoping someone like you would buy it, is that I want to retire, retire from being an Excel guru. I'm here to give away my secrets and help you pull rabbits out of hats. As you become more proficient with Excel, don't be afraid to let people in on how you do it. I had one enduser even keep a card catalogue of all the snippets of code I taught her over the years. Don't be afraid of working yourself out of a job. You're a guru! You can create new dragons to slay.

In fact, you may find out that you actually do sometimes put people out of a job. I've created programs where I turned a process that took a person an entire day or even week to complete into a process that finished in five seconds. Of course, it took time to develop and do all the coding, but these kinds of "tricks" could get you labelled an evil wizard if people's make-work processes go away at the push of a button.

Once you reach this level of Excel wizardry, you become dangerous to some people. They may even blame your tools cause major errors so as to get management to discontinue their use. Yes, someone has actually done that to me. So be as transparent as possible so everyone knows how the magic works. It is unlikely you will be overshadowed by someone who is using some of your tricks because if you're a real guru, you'll have a lot more that they don't yet know.

Besides, if you train people how to understand your tools and processes, you can better integrate so that your things work in tandem and this also makes your skills more valuable as the workplace will be more reliant on your tools.

Nothing is more satisfying for an Excel guru than to walk the office and see your "babies" up on the screens of multiple users. Seeing my spreadsheet creations being used daily and by all levels of staff was very gratifying. I built them to outlast me and some of them are still being used in the various companies for which I have worked.

CHAPTER 7 MARKETING YOURSELF

After learning all this Excel mumbo-jumbo what do you do with it? One goal is to make money from your abilities. But how do you tell people what you know? Most people don't realize the power of Excel. Sure, they may realize the power of cheese but not of a well-crafted spreadsheet and no amount of geek-speak is going to help. You must demonstrate how your knowledge will help them.

I don't know how many jobs I've worked where the interview process was me trying to relate that what I know about Excel is not "*data entry*" but rather "*data understanding*". Perhaps the best method of demonstration is like when you know a friend who has a pickup truck. Yes, like that. Every time you think of hauling oversized objects or moving, you think of that friend. You want people to think of your Excel guru skills in the same way. "*Hey, Bob/Sue knows that computer Excel stuff. Let's ask them to help!*" I apologize if your name is Bob or Sue. I promise I'm not reading your mind.

But this approach to marketing is more for the freelancer. What about when you go for that job interview? You can and should have all the right words on your résumé such as VBA, data analyst, macro, subroutines but will these words mean anything to the interviewer? You need to be prepared to demonstrate your skills. As an Excel guru, don't go to an interview looking for what the employer can do for you but go to the interview to show them what you can do for them. Take a laptop. Show them your skills in action. Almost all businesses that use Excel have a boatload of spreadsheets with data someone is painstakingly sifting through every day. What if you showed them how a simple INDEX MATCH formula could solve their problems? Come with a demo of this. Don't expect them to share their data in the interview. Bring your own "*pickup truck*".

All things to all people

Often, when a person knows a very specific computer task, such as Excel, people will assume they are "good at computers" and will ask the person about all sorts of computer issues. They will begin to see you as their own person "I.T." department. Be careful getting caught up into this scenario – well, unless of course you are good with computers in general and want to be that guy or gal.

No matter how many times you relate that your skills are specific to Excel, you will be called upon to figure out other computer related issues. You may quickly find yourself either in over your head or overwhelmed with other issues. You may need to push back from time to time. However, we have said that everything is a process and process thinking may allow you to see things from a unique perspective. Don't sell yourself short, you may find that you move from being the office Excel guru to chief of operations or implementation because you understand process thinking.

You should be constantly marketing yourself, your skills, your solutions. Look for processes that could be greatly improved by your Excel tools. You may even have to initiate the process with a mockup before being asked so that you can present it. People don't always know what they want until shown.

Your process thinking approach will expand into other areas of your life. I've even had people become annoyed with me because they think I'm keeping a log of everything they say or do around me, but it's merely the way I've organized comments and actions so that they are better recalled.

Once you begin to think in this way, developing the spreadsheet or VBA project will become easier. People will begin to rely upon and even expect your assistance in things that are not even Excel related. It is here where you will need to decide if you want to market yourself as more than the Excel guru. Just be careful not to become more than you are. So many people believe their own press. The fall from a pedestal too high will hurt more than you think.

Be truthful with your abilities. Not just with perspective customers but with yourself. This is a crucial time. You are at the moment where you might very well add more skills to your profile. You might learn other computer languages that are in demand. Now is the time to decide if you want to be merely self-taught and market those skills yourself or be certified and let the certifications speak for you.

The questions to ask yourself are about money; investment and return and about commitment and dedication. Do you want your skills to turn into money and how much money and time will you have to invest?

Are you certifiable?

Or rather, do you want to be certified in Microsoft products? It could open doors but is not necessary to land a good job.

Certifications within the Microsoft Certification Program include the following credentials:

- **Microsoft Technology Associate (MTA)**
- **Microsoft Certified Solutions Associate (MCSA)**
- **Microsoft Certified Solutions Expert (MCSE)**
- **Microsoft Solutions Developer (MCSD)**
- **Microsoft Office Specialist (MOS)**

Most likely, you will want to obtain the Microsoft Office Specialist certification. Just keep in mind the Microsoft Certified Professional (MCP) certification is not part of the MOS. You may want to obtain some of the other certifications to ensure your MCP status. Orrrr if all this seems pointless to you and you just want to prove your abilities to people as you go, then skip all this.

But if you want to learn more about the various certifications that Microsoft offers, do a search or go to this link:
https://docs.microsoft.com/en-us/learn/certifications/

Marketing your certifications are as easy as a doctor with all the letters behind his or her name, however they might not mean much to a perspective employer who just sees a bunch of letters. Again, you'll need to decide if the investment is worth it. There is such a thing as getting passed over for being "overly qualified". The employer may think you will become bored with the positions they are offering and not even contact you.

Ultimately, you will still have to prove yourself and many companies now have technology specialists within the management team that can spot inflated resumes. Interviewers are often more interested in whether you will be able to mesh well with their team.

Employers look for a self-motivated problem solver with "spark" over a long list of credentials. They will work with you if you need extra on-job education but will not long employ people who have all the checkmarks on paper but will not adapt and grow within the position.

So, the best way to market yourself is to market yourself as:

- **A self-motivated problem solver**
- **Adaptable to changes**
- **A team player**
- **A potential leader**

Another route to marketing yourself is to build a name for yourself in the Excel community. Yes, there is such a thing. Remember those Excel forums and websites I keep pushing? If you have visited, you'll see some of the same people answering most of the questions. Spend some time helping others, for free. If you believe in karma, I'm sure it will come back to you.

With the advent of social media, the venues for self-promotion are limitless. While it is not my intention to become the next Excel YouTube star, you certainly could. But keep the videos short; maybe 10 minutes or less. Something a person could watch while getting their oil changed. Keep the content well defined so a person can watch the topic of interest. Get to the point instead of long introductions. Have you noticed how many movies no longer have long credits displayed at the beginning of the movie? That's so pre-1980s.

Next, you might consider writing a book. Yeah you. You can do it. I did it and you read nearly twelve thousand words so far. The book should be engaging and fun. Let's admit it, Excel is boring if not intimidating to many people, so we need to put them at ease. Make them think we're "normal" people even if we're not.

Before you know it, you could be driving around in a luxury car with a vanity license plate that reads XL001 or something like that. Being an Excel guru is grueling and unappreciated work but hey, someone has to do it. Take one for the team!

CHAPTER 8 TRANSCEND

Someday you will move beyond being an expert, which is really just an amateur who has messed up lots of times and learned from mistakes. When you reach this point, you will know it. Maybe you were an Excel guru before you started reading this book. Maybe you are a guru in some other field, and you are beginning to feel this urge to transcend, to move beyond it and unto something else. After all, I was a nerdy data analyst dude that now loves to do landscape art and paint strange pictures with lots of swirling circles.

So, this book isn't just about helping a person become an Excel guru but is about helping them incorporate all of that into their lives. All the talk of process thinking and organizing your mind to think in patterns is bigger than Bill Gates' little invention. You didn't know what you were getting into when you started reading this book, did you?

A spreadsheet is an excellent analogy of the mind. With all its little cells, boxes waiting to be filled with data. All of its relational lists and sets. If this is how you are thinking, you truly are an Excel guru. Maybe stop reading a moment and just appreciate a blank worksheet.

Now imagine the cells not filled with mere numbers but with statements, sentences, questions asked. Are they cells or boxes or bricks to build a structure?

If you program in languages beyond VBA you no doubt see the connection between them all. They truly are more than IF THEN DO THIS conditional statements. You might even imagine a day when computers program themselves. Already, the autocorrect and the predictive search engines are a type of self-programming. Imagine a world where computers have so analyzed the human patterns that computers can predict what we want before we even express it. Scary yes.

This is why I am trying to transcend above the process thinking and organized mind to something more. But what is beyond those things? Is it really about just letting all that go and getting back to nature? Should we really be running naked in the woods? Ummmm…I hope not. The transcendence should include all the things that got us here.

So, as you move in and out of different areas of expertise you should keep an eye on the bigger things. It would be sad if you worked at the ABC Corporation all your life and became the Excel or Python guru and at some point, passed away, lonely with just the memory of your one room apartment and loyal lap cat. Okay okay, I'm making it more dramatic than it probably will be, but you get the point.

Experts in any field often find themselves typecast or boxed into it. They cannot easily move beyond it. People expect them to always play that role. A true guru knows not to take themselves too seriously. It is almost as if they happened upon their skill rather than having dedicated the time and effort to hone it.

Maybe your transcendence will be more like transference. You will simply transfer all the process thinking and organized mind to another skillset.

But sometimes I feel like Excel is leaving me behind. I dabble in it some but the days when I would literally dream about formulas and subroutines is fading. If you want to remain an Excel guru forever, you will need to keep practicing the art. Like Kungfu, you will need to spar, not merely dance a kata.

The next few pages I will offer some challenges for you to practice your skills. It will most likely require you to do some research. I hope you accept the challenge.

Circular Reference

. One of the most annoying problems faced by Excel users is the circular reference. This is, as you might know referring to the same cell or range as the question and result. It is the classic, *"who created the creator?"* dilemma.

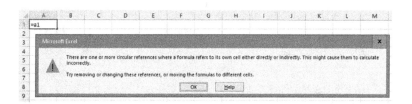

As an Excel guru, can you solve this issue? Can you figure out a way to refer to the same cell or range as the question and the answer? Use named-ranges or helper cells, or VBA. Whatever you need to see if you can solve it. Maybe there is no solution but the adventure is in the trying.

Everything is a subset of something else

In computing languages this is typically called "properties". This is especially true in object-oriented languages where a thing is an object such as a worksheet is a subset of a workbook and a workbook is a subset of the Excel application and on and on.

But think how this is true in general. A creature can be classified into a subset or group such mammal, reptile and so forth. From there, each species can be further sub classified, such as live birth, egg laying and on and on. The same is true with Excel. Almost everything has a property which can be set, usually to true or false, 1 or 0 or to contain or store data such as a string of text or a value.

For example, each workbook has a lot of properties that can be changed to control the color of the tab, whether the tab is the active tab and so forth.

Open a new workbook, right click on sheet1 and VIEW CODE. This will launch the VBA editor.

In the editing box (the large white box to the right), input **sheet1.** (with the period at the end).

You should see something like the following:

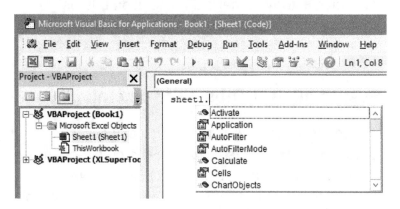

Notice the scroll down of alphabetical properties that begin with ACTIVATE. Scroll through and see some of the properties that can be set on a worksheet.

Many of the properties have sub-properties just like we could classify human eyes like this:

eyes

.count = 2
.color = "green"
.shape = "oval"

These properties could be changed depending on what we want or what actually is. The same is true in Excel. Look for the properties in all things and understand how they work. This is the epitome of process thinking. Think about the process and how it works and how you can best affect it. This approach will help with more than just Excel. Everything is an object with parts or properties. Whether we're talking about governments, ice-cream, or computer applications; everything has parts we can affect and change to change the overall behavior of the object.

CustomProperties

As you begin your transcendence beyond being a guru, what if you could go beyond the prefabricated properties and instead make your own properties? Excel allows you to do this with a process canned CustomProperties. You can create your own properties, define, and set them as you wish. You then can access and manipulate these properties as needed.

Look up CustomProperties and Excel on Google or your favorite search engine then try to create, access, and change these properties. The good thing about this process is that these properties stay with the object as you share the object with other people. This means, they don't need to enable macros or such to allow your properties to work, unless of course you are using a macro to manipulate the properties.

Think about how CustomProperties could come in handy. It could store a list or be an initialization process that must happen before your masterpiece workbook functions.

Formulas to Functions

Another great exercise for an Excel guru is to try to make a worksheet formula work inside a VBA module. While in theory, there should be an equivalent and often shorter way to do the same thing in VBA as you do in a worksheet formula, there may be instances where that is not true. You may know how to perfectly execute something in a worksheet formula but have no idea how to make it work in VBA.

But you can make most, if not all worksheet formulas "evaluate" in VBA. It's often cumbersome and a bit tricky since it requires wrapping parts of the formula in double quotation marks.

An example may look like this:

Sheet1.formula = "=A1=F2"

Or more complex:

hitrow = Application.Match(Itemtofind.Value, Workbooks(Comprange.Parent.Parent.Name).Sheets(Comprange.Parent.Name).Range(Comprange.Address), 0)

85

Notice how I've used the worksheet formula of =match(matchitem, range, 0) and turned it into a VBA line that finds an item in a specific worksheet range address. Is there a less complex way to do this? Probably but knowing how to get at properties and sub sub sub sub properties is a very powerful ability as an Excel guru.

User Defined Functions UDF

It may be a little late in this book to be talking about User Defined Functions, but again this book isn't trying to teach you everything about Excel. It is trying to get you to think like an Excel guru.

If you don't already know, in VBA there are predefined functions that are like the formulas in a worksheet. For example, in a worksheet you would use

=value("2") to convert a string of text into a value but in VBA you would use **newval = val("2")** defining the result as newval or whatever you want it to be called. The difference is between the name of the formula and function. The worksheet calls it *value* and VBA calls it *val*. So, there is a bit of learning of which version to use and when.

Now, add to that, Excel allows you to create your own functions and then use or "call" them within your modules. Maybe you want to always convert the name "Roderick" into the word "Dork" but you wouldn't want to do this each time you write a module so instead you run the resultant string through your user defined function. Something like this:

For a worksheet formula, first find RODERICK in the text, in this case cell A1. (Put the formula in some other cell other than A1 and type, "*Roderick is a nerd*" in cell A1) Notice that since FIND is case-sensitive, we have made the entire string in A1 upper case then look for RODERICK in the string. This formula simply finds the first position of the instance of RODERICK in A1. It will return the position number.

=FIND("RODERICK",UPPER(A1))

Now how do you change all instances of Roderick into Dork? Type "*Roderick is a nerd, yes Roderick is a nerd*" into cell A1. Then place this formula into another cell:

=SUBSTITUTE(UPPER(A1),"RODERICK","Dork")

Now you see how to do it in a formula but what about a VBA UDF? Notice how I am showing you how to do it both ways and how to understand how each works.

87

In the VBA, type the following. See how it is NOT a subroutine but rather a *function*.

Function roddork(orgstr As String)

roddork = WorksheetFunction.Substitute(UCase(orgstr), "RODERICK", "Dork")

End Function

Here, I used a variation of the worksheet formula. You can do that with most worksheet formulas and use them in subroutines or functions. It is a bit clunky and lazy and will probably get you thrown out of the black-tie social club when Excel snobs gather for tea and crumpets. So, I'm going to show you another way.

The "right" way to do it would be:

```
Function roddork(orgstr As String)

roddork = replace(UCase(orgstr), "RODERICK", "Dork")

End Function
```

This way, you aren't using a worksheet function to do VBA work. But who says what the "right" way to do something is, if it works right?

Note here again, in the formula we used **UPPER** but in the VBA we used **UCASE**. This little variation in how to accomplish things is a bit annoying at first. Google is your friend…well, unless you are trying to post controversial yet factual things to social media and then you'll probably get banned. See picture on previous page for what an "official fact-checker" may look like.

You can call the UDF in a worksheet by using **=roddork(cell address)** or **=roddork(string of text)**.

Or in a subroutine by assigning it a variable:

newtext = roddork(cell address or string of text)

CHAPTER 9 THE NTH DEGREE

Now we're at the last chapter. Do you feel like a guru yet? Did you learn anything? Do you feel like the money you spent was well worth it? What kind of author talks about such a taboo topic? This one! This book is my swan song, my encore, my exiting the Excel stage. It's time for you to take up the fight!

Anyone who has worked with me on Excel projects or benefited from one of my creations knows that my "tools" work and often stand the test of time. I know for certain that some Excel tools I created five and ten years ago are still being used today. I'm not saying this to brag or pat myself on the back. I want you to realize how important your work could be. Give it thought. Design it to last. So many things today are following the planned obsolescence model of a predefined failure point. Your cell phone or your car was designed to breakdown at a certain age, so you'll buy the next model. It is time to be part of the Nth Degree that pushes into the future. I'm not trying to be melodramatic here but if you're going to tell people you read my book and got ideas from it, I want it to be quality work. I am concerned about your reputation and mine.

Now is the time to reflect on everything you have read. Was this the kind of book you expected? Are you going to just stuff it between all your other self-help and technical guides? Are you going to share it with family and friends?

What kind of book asks you if you are a different person now? How presumptuous. But this is exactly what I am asking you. As I kept telling you all through the book, this isn't just another Excel book full of snippets and examples but rather it is a book written by a guru for apprentices and other gurus.

Life Formula

I want you to look at life like conditional formulas. I didn't learn all this just to be someone's little nerd nor did you. You might have bought this book to help you be better at Excel but now you can be better at life. Maybe you'll say *"But I don't want that from you Rod. Just show me how to do Excel!"* Too late, you read this far already. There is no escape from the metamorphosis. You will begin to see "Excel" in everything; music, art, nature, human behavior. Everything can be categorized and measured… until it can't.

Process thinking and Organized Mind

For the last chapter, we will discuss what you should expect next in your Excel career. The next chapter of your life will either show more opportunities to use your experience with Excel or you will begin to also exit the stage and move onto other things.

I've known people who have used Excel for almost two decades and their expertise level is still at A1+B1. They either had no need or desire to move further. Which kind of person will you be or are you?

Alternatives to Excel

Microsoft Excel has been in existence since its Macintosh version in 1985 and its Windows version in 1987 but many other developers have tried to compete with the office place staple.

OpenOffice is now more or less defunct but was one of the first serious opensource contenders to Excel. While it is still being developed, its interoperability is less than stellar and many of its nuances discourage ex-Excel users.

LibreOffice is a branch-off of the OpenOffice project and its developers have attempted to make it more compatible with Excel. One advantage of the suite package is that the Microsoft Word alternative called *Write*, can possibly edit PDF files.

Google Sheets is a web only version of a spreadsheet program but at the time of this writing had no "macro" or subroutine abilities. You can upload Excel workbooks that have basic formulas and they will still work.

There are many other alternatives which may be fun to work with but have yet to replace Excel.

See https://en.wikipedia.org/wiki/List_of_spreadsheet_software

If you plan to work with an alternative to Excel or offer one to a client as a low cost or no cost solution, just realize all of these alternatives have major limitations. These alternatives may become a nightmare for you. I've actually worked for one company that had Excel for the management and some knockoff alternative for the rest of the staff but expected me to make sure the workbooks behaved the same when shared. I never could get the colors to match from Excel to the knockoff and it caused a lot of confusion when people were trying to use cell colors as indicators.

If you are going to transcend to the Nth Degree of Excel knowledge, not only will you need to learn the secret Excel handshake and chant but also you will need to have an early version of Excel which still contains easter egg hidden programs. Yes, that's right. Early versions had little hidden programs like maze games and racing if you knew the right thing to make it start.

See
https://www.techrepublic.com/pictures/look-back-at-microsoft-excel-easter-eggs/

But seriously, to be an Excel expert you should learn some of the nerdier stuff about Excel, like the alternatives and how they are different. Get some of those freeware alternatives and toy around with them. Maybe you will find you like them better for personal use.

Another thing I learned working in an international environment is that Excel in other countries might not operate the same way it does in the USA. Some of the worksheet and VBA functions are translated into the host language. For example, here is a short list of English to Spanish equivalents

Full Source: https://www.excel-function-translation.com/index.php?page=english-spanish.html

Function in English	Function in Spanish
ADDRESS	DIRECCION
COLUMN	COLUMNA
COLUMNS	COLUMNAS
HLOOKUP	BUSCARH
HYPERLINK	HIPERVINCULO
INDEX	INDICE
INDIRECT	INDIRECTO
LOOKUP	BUSCAR
MATCH	COINCIDIR
OFFSET	DESREF
ROW	FILA
ROWS	FILAS
TRANSPOSE	TRANSPONER
VLOOKUP	BUSCARV

You can see how this could cause problems when trying to interact with non-English Excel users.

I want to leave you with your head swirling with all the possibilities and applications of process thinking and an organized mind. I want to be reading some article in the future of some Elon Musk or Marissa Mayer who quote this weird little book by some Excel nerd as an inspiration. But for now, I have chickens to feed and a rooster to dodge. I have a garden to tend and a pond to gaze. Now YOU are the Excel guru. It's your time.

ABOUT THE AUTHOR

RODERICK EDWARDS is the author of books as varied as a fictional account of a person living in a deserted world to an autobiographic about his adoption and reunion, a book about the Universe, to a book about Government overthrow and then this one to help you be better at Excel.

Find out more at
amazon.com/author/roderickedwards

Or visit rodericke.com

OTHER BOOKS BY RODERICK

- How to Overthrow a Government

https://www.amazon.com/dp/1653337893

- The Universe: Of Every Religion and None

https://www.amazon.com/dp/1696882419

- Togethermore: Rejection and Reunion

https://www.amazon.com/dp/1688917055

- PVE: A Survivor's Journal

https://www.amazon.com/dp/1980491496

- ONE: Exploration of Individualism

https://www.amazon.com/dp/B01LPBOKO4

- About Preterism: The End is Past

https://www.amazon.com/dp/1079955798

SEE ALSO, many of these titles are available as AUDIOBOOKS!!!

audible.com/author/B07B9R59Q2

CAN I ASK A FAVOR?

If you enjoyed this book, found it useful or otherwise then I'd really appreciate it if you would post a short review on Amazon. I do read all the reviews personally so that I can continually write what people are wanting.

If you'd like to leave a review then please visit the link below:

amazon.com/author/roderickedwards

Thanks for your support!

INDEX